Cell Phone Addiction

Bradley Steffens

ReferencePoint Press®

San Diego, CA

© 2020 ReferencePoint Press, Inc.
Printed in the United States

For more information, contact:
ReferencePoint Press, Inc.
PO Box 27779
San Diego, CA 92198
www.ReferencePointPress.com

LIBRARY OF CONGRESS CATALOGING-IN-PUBLICATION DATA

Name: Steffens, Bradley, 1955– author.
Title: Cell Phone Addiction/by Bradley Steffens.
Description: San Diego, CA: ReferencePoint Press, Inc., [2020] | Series:
   Emerging Issues in Public Health | Audience: Grade 9 to 12. |
   Includes bibliographical references and index.
Identifiers: LCCN 2018051669 (print) | LCCN 2018051914 (ebook) | ISBN
   9781682826669 (eBook) | ISBN 9781682826652 (hardback)
Subjects: LCSH: Internet addiction—Juvenile literature. | Cell
   phones—Social aspects—Juvenile literature.
Classification: LCC RC569.5.I54 (ebook) | LCC RC569.5.I54 S74 2020 (print) |
   DDC 616.85/84—dc23
LC record available at https://lccn.loc.gov/2018051669

CONTENTS

A Growing Danger

Concerned about the behavior they had observed in their classrooms, professors at two business schools in Italy and France designed a simple one-day experiment to examine how cell phone use is affecting the lives of young people. They asked graduate students at the University of Bologna in Italy and at the Kedge Business School in Bordeaux, France, to suspend all cell phone use for a twenty-four-hour period and keep a journal about their experience. A total of 153 students participated in the Surviving a Day Without Smartphones project between 2015 and 2017. The results were disturbing. "For many, the strongest feeling was anxiety," the professors explain. "Students felt anxious about missing something important."[1] Many project participants found that not having a cell phone gave them more free time, but they found this disorienting. Without a smartphone, one student wrote in his diary, "my breakfast was too short and I did not know what to do next."[2] Another was frustrated because he could not use his cell phone to fill the time as he commuted to school. He described the bus and train trip as "the longest time of my life."[3] A French student also felt a void, writing, "I was not capable of doing nothing. I was thinking about my phone all the time."[4] The lack of a cell phone made some students feel vulnerable and afraid. "I was feeling uncomfortable, with no possibility to hide behind the phone screen,"[5] wrote one student. An Italian student expressed fears about losing touch with people and being excluded. "I am not receiving messages, photos, emails, likes, comments, etc.," she wrote. "It feels as if no one is willing to interact with me, thinking about me! I am alone!"[6]

The Surviving a Day Without Smartphones project confirms what psychologists, researchers, parents, teachers, and students have observed worldwide: more and more people are dependent on their cell phones for feelings of well-being. "My Smartphone is literally my life," a focus group participant told researchers from Nottingham Trent University in Nottingham, England, in 2018. "Self-professed addict. This is my calendar, this is how I communicate with everybody, how I organise my life, how I get up in the morning. It is my adult pacifier."[7]

The Impacts on Mental Health

High use of cell phones is having noticeable effects on individuals and society. Researchers have found that heavy cell phone use is chemically rewiring the brain, producing chemicals that slow down the brain and suppressing chemicals that speed it up. Heavy cell phone use has been associated with reduced capacity for concentration, impaired cognitive thinking, less encoding of memories, and a loss of impulse control. Even moderate cell phone use is negatively affecting relationships between parents and children, friends, and romantic partners, according to mental health professionals.

There is mounting scientific evidence that the round-the-clock bombardment of cell phone notifications, text messages, and social media activity is affecting the mental health of cell phone users, especially teenagers. An August 2018 survey by the Pew Research Center found that 56 percent of teens associate the absence of their cell phone with at least one of these three emotions: loneliness, being upset, or feeling anxious. Researchers at San Diego State University have found a correlation between high cell phone use—more than five hours a day—and increased rates of depression,

"It's not an exaggeration to describe iGen [people born between 1995 and 2012] as being on the brink of the worst mental-health crisis in decades. Much of this deterioration can be traced to their phones."[8]

—Jean M. Twenge, a psychology professor at San Diego State University suicidal thoughts, and suicide in adolescents. "It's not an exaggeration to describe iGen [people born between 1995 and 2012] as being on the brink of the worst mental-health crisis in decades," writes Jean M. Twenge, the lead author of the study. "Much of this deterioration can be traced to their phones."[8]

Public Safety

Cell phone distractions are affecting not only individuals but also the public at large. A study by the National Safety Council, a nonprofit organization promoting health and safety, found that 26 percent of automobile crashes are the result of drivers being distracted by their mobile devices. The Department for Transport, a government agency responsible for transportation matters in the United Kingdom, reports that people are twice as likely to crash when texting than when driving drunk.

Pedestrian traffic fatalities are also on the rise. Pedestrian deaths (from all causes) increased by 27 percent between 2007 and 2017. "Drivers distracted by their devices are a well-documented, rising cause of traffic crashes, but there are a growing number of pedestrians, too, who can become oblivious to traffic around them,"[9] says Maureen Vogel, a spokesperson for the Governors Highway Safety Association, a nonprofit organization concerned with highway safety.

Addiction

Despite the many dangers of heavy cell phone use, increasing numbers of users cannot resist the impulse to check their cell phones many times per hour throughout the day, every day. Mental health professionals are beginning to refer to this behavior as cell phone addiction, which is defined by researchers in the field as "an inability to regulate one's use of the mobile phone, which eventually involves negative consequences in daily life."[10]

Students Worldwide Feel Lost Without Their Cell Phones

Researchers at the University of Maryland asked college students from ten different countries to give up their cell phones for twenty-four hours and describe how it felt to be unplugged during that time. Although the students said they could see the benefits of unplugging, their answers were overwhelmingly negative. Feelings of addiction and distress ranked high among their various emotional responses. Cumulatively, the negative feelings of not having access to cell phones for a twenty-four-hour period far outweighed the positive feelings. The University of Maryland study is similar to one done in Italy and France.

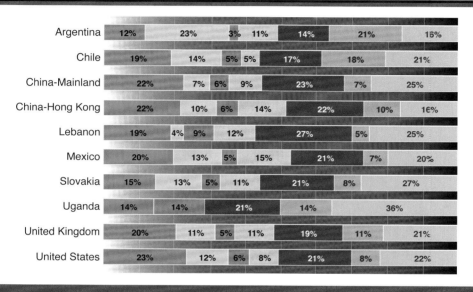

Country	Addiction	Failure	Boredom	Confusion	Distress	Isolation	Benefits of unplugging
Argentina	12%	23%	3%	11%	14%	21%	16%
Chile	19%	14%	5%	5%	17%	18%	21%
China-Mainland	22%	7%	6%	9%	23%	7%	25%
China-Hong Kong	22%	10%	6%	14%	22%	10%	16%
Lebanon	19%	4%	9%	12%	27%	5%	25%
Mexico	20%	13%	5%	15%	21%	7%	20%
Slovakia	15%	13%	5%	11%	21%	8%	27%
Uganda	14%	14%		21%	14%		36%
United Kingdom	20%	11%	5%	11%	19%	11%	21%
United States	23%	12%	6%	8%	21%	8%	22%

Source: the world UNPLUGGED, "Going 24 Hours Without Media," 2018. https://theworldunplugged.wordpress.com.

Cell phone addiction, sometimes also referred to as overuse or dependence, is a new and growing public health concern. Oxford University researchers say that cell phone addiction is reported by up to 38 percent of cell phone users worldwide. The rate is even higher among teens and young adults. Half of individuals in these age groups say they feel addicted to their devices. As they age and more children are born into a cell phone world, the number of cell phone addicts will only increase unless effective public health programs are established.

CHAPTER ONE

The Making of a Public Health Crisis

The cell phone represents an amazing advance in technology. To appreciate its development, imagine a mother going to her daughter's gymnastics meet in 2001. The proud mom carries a digital camera to take pictures of her daughter and her daughter's teammates. She has a video camera to tape her daughter's routines. She has a cell phone that allows her to make voice calls and send text messages. A busy executive, she has a handheld computer (a PDA, or personal digital assistant) that allows her to send and receive e-mails, compose memos, schedule meetings on an electronic calendar, and even browse the Internet. A music lover, she carries the newly released iPod digital music player, so she can listen to her favorite music as she watches. Less than ten years later, the woman's daughter, a college graduate and executive herself, is at her four-year-old daughter's first tumbling class. Like her mother, the young woman is taking photos and videos of her daughter, checking e-mail, sending texts, listening to music, and browsing the Internet. But instead of using five different devices, she does it all with one—her cell phone. In fact, her cell phone takes clearer pictures and video than her mother's cameras did, and it allows her to upload the images to social media websites in real time. That is a technical revolution.

Usage

Thanks to the multitude of functions they offer, cell phones are the most quickly adopted technology in history, rising from 10 percent of US households in 1994 to 95 percent of households in 2014. According to a 2018 survey by the Pew Research Center, 95 percent of Americans now own a cell phone, with 77 percent saying they own an Internet-capable smartphone. The average age when children get their first phone is now just ten years old. More than 5.1 billion people—about 67 percent of the world's population—have cell phones. About two-thirds (3.3 billion) of these phones are smartphones.

With its rich array of functions, including the ability to stream not just music but also videos, movies, and live television, the modern cell phone is more than just a communications device. It is a powerful computer and handheld media center. Not surprisingly, people are spending increasing amounts of time using their cell phones. According to eMarketer, a media analysis company, US adults spent an average of 3 hours, 35 minutes per day on mobile devices in 2018—a 70 percent increase since 2013. The firm predicted that the average US adult would spend more time using a cell phone than watching television in 2019. Most teens already do. According to Common Sense Media, the average American teenager with a smartphone spends more than 4.5 hours a day on the device, not counting texting and talking.

A Reward System

Part of the problem for both teens and adults is that cell phone apps are designed to keep people involved with their cell phones. Many cell phone apps link a user's actions to receiving rewards, but the rewards vary. This system, known as intermittent variable rewards, is the same technique used to keep gamblers playing slot machines, hoping that the next pull of a lever will result in a prize. Cell phone apps provide intermittent variable rewards by feeding the user notifications and messages. Justin Rosenstein, a former Facebook engineer who created the first "like" button, calls these rewards "bright dings of pseudo-pleasure."[11] The anticipation of the reward makes it hard for people to turn off their device, to stop notifications, or to unsubscribe to a service. Intermittent variable rewards maximize interest in the app to the point of addictiveness. "Smartphones are useful tools," says Loren Brichter, the software designer who invented the pull-to-refresh mechanism for an app that Twitter eventually acquired. "But they're addictive. Pull-to-refresh is addictive. Twitter is addictive. These are not good things. When I was working on them, it was not something I was mature enough to think about. I'm not saying I'm mature now, but I'm a little bit more mature, and I regret the downsides."[12]

People are also hooked by the social aspects of cell phone use. Sometimes the intermittent variable reward is social media approval—likes, loves, shares, and retweets on their posts. Many people also feel obligated to tag others, share news and achievements, and to quickly respond to messages, especially when delivery notifications show the sender that they have read them. The continuous loop of receiving, reading, and responding to alerts creates an endless loop of involvement and a fear of missing out. A recent Common Sense Media survey found that 72 percent of teens and 48 percent of parents feel the need to immediately respond to texts, social networking messages, and other notifications. "Too many of us have become slaves to the devices that were supposed to free us," writes Jane E. Brody, a health columnist for the *New York Times*. "Instead, we're constantly bombarded by bells, buzzers and chimes that alert us to messages we feel compelled to view and respond to immediately."[13]

> "Smartphones are useful tools. But they're addictive. Pull-to-refresh is addictive. Twitter is addictive. These are not good things."[12]
>
> —Loren Brichter, the inventor of the pull-to-refresh cell phone feature

Portability

The portability of the cell phone makes the addictive tendencies more dangerous. A person might be mesmerized by a slot machine, but he or she cannot carry one around. Gambling addicts may spend all of their time at casinos, but moderately affected people walk away from the slot machines at some point. The portability of cell phones means that the reward system is always

Cell phones are the most quickly adopted technological innovation in history. In 1994 only about 10 percent of US households possessed a cell phone, but by 2018, 95 percent of Americans reported having one.

within reach. People who otherwise would not develop a reward-based habit find themselves checking their phones constantly. "All of us are jacked into this system," says Tristan Harris, a former Google employee. "All of our minds can be hijacked. Our choices are not as free as we think they are."[14]

The combined effects of intermittent rewards and portability are staggering. According to an app developed by technology research firm dscout, cell phone users touch their cell phones an average of 2,617 times a day to check on social media updates, read text messages, make calls, and perform other tasks. In a dscout study, users registered more than 5,400 cell phone touches per day. "Per year, that's nearly one million touches on average—and two million for the less restrained among us,"

> "All of us are jacked into this system. All of our minds can be hijacked. Our choices are not as free as we think they are."[14]
>
> —Tristan Harris, a former Google employee

A Problem for Cell Phone Researchers

Scientific studies involving the effects of cell phones are hampered by the fact that nearly everyone owns a cell phone. When scientists design an experiment, they often work with two groups of subjects. The first group, known as the test group, is normally exposed to something; the second group, known as the control, is not. For example, when testing drugs, the test group receives a drug, but the control group does not. However, the control group receives a placebo, which is a drug look-alike that has no effect. This is done because a subject who believes he or she is receiving treatment (but is not) sometimes feels better, a phenomenon known as the placebo effect. Tests that use placebos are known as blind tests because the subjects do not know if they are receiving the treatment or the placebo.

It is nearly impossible to find anyone who has not already been exposed to a cell phone who could serve in a control group. In addition, scientists cannot conduct a blind test because it would be impossible to fool people into using a fake cell phone. Even if researchers could find people who have not been exposed to cell phones, it would be unethical to expose them to something that might cause cancer.

Because of these difficulties, cell phone studies can only compare people who use cell phones a lot with people who use them less. These studies have a problem, too. People who use cell phones heavily might have a different lifestyle than those who do not. As a result, their health might already be different.

writes Michael Winnick, the founder and chief executive officer of dscout. "We're definitely letting our fingers do the walking, and they're doing marathons. Each tap and swipe feels small and harmless—just a tiny fraction of our brain power and physical effort. But at these volumes, have the interactions become an onerous load?"[15]

Diet, Exercise, and Sleep

High levels of involvement with any device is bound to have consequences in daily life, and experts say this is the case with cell phones. High levels of cell phone use can affect the user's diet and exercise regimen, according to Erica Kenney and Steven Gortmaker of the Harvard T.H. Chan School of Public Health in Boston. In 2017 Kenney and Gortmaker surveyed 24,800 US high school students about their use of cell phones and other screen devices. They also asked the students about their health behaviors, including their consumption of sugar-sweetened beverages, physical activity, sleep, and weight and height. About 20 percent of the respondents used cell phones and other screen devices (not counting television) more than five hours a day. The researchers found that such usage was associated with daily consumption of sugary drinks, inadequate physical activity, and inadequate sleep. "Using smartphones, tablets, computers, and videogames is associated with several obesity risk factors,"[16] write Kenney and Gortmaker.

Cell phone use also affects sleep patterns. The dscout study found that over a five-day period 87 percent of participants checked their phones at least once between midnight and 5 a.m. Other studies have found a correlation between screen times and sleep patterns. Teens who spend five or more hours a day on electronic devices are 51 percent more likely to get less than seven hours of sleep than are teens who spend less than one hour on the devices, according to psychologist Jean M. Twenge. Scientists at Réseau-Morphée, a sleep clinic in Garches, France, also report a link between cell phone use and sleep deprivation. A 2017 survey of 786 teens (408 females and 368 males) found that more than 85 percent of the teens had cell phones in their bedrooms, and more than half (52 percent) regularly used their electronic devices after bedtime. Many teens even used their cell phones if they woke up at night, with 15 percent sending texts and 11 percent using social media.

"Each tap and swipe feels small and harmless—just a tiny fraction of our brain power and physical effort. But at these volumes, have the interactions become an onerous load?"[15]

—Michael Winnick, the founder and chief executive officer of dscout

Cell phone use affects behaviors including diet, exercise, and sleep habits. One study found that 87 percent of participants checked their phones at least once between midnight and 5 a.m. over a five-day period.

The effects of sleep deprivation are significant. Sleep deprivation is a risk factor for several diseases, including obesity, diabetes, cardiovascular disease, and depression. The teenagers in the French study who did not get the recommended nine hours of sleep per night had a harder time getting to sleep than those who did get enough sleep. Thirty-three percent of the sleep-deprived teens took more than an hour to fall asleep compared to just 9 percent of those who were not sleep deprived. The sleep-deprived teens also had a harder time getting up in the morning, were more likely to fight sleepiness during the day, had less energy, and reported greater irritability and feelings of sadness. "Access to social media and especially a cell phone in teenagers' bedrooms is associated with a reduction in sleep time during the school week with negative effects on daily functioning and mood,"[17] write the researchers.

Hand, Neck, and Shoulder Pain

Excessive cell phone use is also linked to various kinds of physical pain, especially in the neck, shoulders, and hands. University researchers in Turkey found that cell phone overuse enlarges the median nerve in the hand—the nerve that enables the thumb, palm, and first three fingers to move. This enlargement causes pain in the thumb and decreases pinch strength and hand functions. Researchers in South Korea discovered that text messaging, which is one of the most frequently used cell phone apps, is a main contributing factor in the occurrence of neck pain experienced by heavy smartphone users. Texting increases the angle that the user's neck is bent, which can cause pain over an extended period of time.

The latter finding is supported by a 2018 study conducted by researchers at the University of Queensland in Australia. Using a process known as kinematics, these researchers used electronic sensors to create three-dimensional renderings of the neck and spine positions of thirty-seven people as they used their cell phones. The study participants performed three tasks while wearing the sensors: texting on a smartphone with one hand, texting with two hands, and typing on a desktop computer. Nineteen of the participants were healthy, but eighteen had chronic neck and shoulder pain. The researchers found that cell phone texting significantly increased the bending, or flexion, of the spine. Two-handed texting was associated with increased flexion of the cervical vertebrae, just below the skull, and one-handed texting was associated with an off-center neck posture. "Both text-entry methods are not favorable in terms of spinal postures," write the researchers. "This study suggests that altered kinematics may be associated with pain."[18]

Cell Phones and Cancer

The most serious concern about cell phone use is its possible link to cancer. In May 2011 the International Agency for Research on Cancer (IARC) classified radio frequency (RF) energy, the type of radiation emitted by cell phones, as a possible carcinogen. That meant the connection between cell phone radiation and brain tumors was not certain, but it could not be ruled out. In 2017 an Italian court ruled that a worker's brain tumor was the result of excessive cell phone use. Italy's nonprofit National Institute for Insurance against Accidents at Work (INAIL), which insures workers who become disabled, had denied executive Roberto Romeo benefits related to his brain tumor. Romeo sued to prove that his brain tumor was caused by work-related cell phone use. "I had no choice but to use my mobile to talk to colleagues and organise work—for fifteen years I was calling all the time, from home, in the car," said Romeo. "I started to have the feeling of my right ear being blocked all the time and the tumour was diagnosed in 2010. Happily, it was benign but I can no longer hear anything because they had to remove my acoustic nerve."[19] The court found the tumor to be work related and ordered INAIL to pay Romeo a lifetime pension.

In 2018 two major studies—one by researchers at the National Toxicology Program, a federal interagency group under the National Institutes of Health (NIH), and one by investigators at the Ramazzini Institute in Italy—both found an association between cell phone radiation and an increased risk for cancer. The study by the NIH was the largest investigation of RF radiation and cancer in rodents ever undertaken in the United States. The scientists tested three thousand rats and mice of both sexes for two years, exposing them to ten-minute doses of RF radiation followed by ten minutes of no radiation for a total of nine hours of radiation a day. The mice were not affected, and neither were the female rats. However, the male rats developed a rare tumor of the heart, known as a schwannoma, at statistically higher rates than did the control animals that were not exposed to the radiation. The researchers also found slightly higher levels of gliomas—tumors that grow in the brain—in the rats that received RF radiation. The researchers concluded there was clear evidence linking RF radiation with heart schwannomas and some evidence linking it to gliomas of the brain.

The Italian study found similar results. In that study, twenty-five hundred rats were exposed to different levels of what is known as far-field radiation, the kind of wireless RF radiation emitted by cell phone towers, cell phones, and other wireless devices. The rats received doses of radiation for nineteen hours a day from the time they were fetuses until they died of natural causes. The male rats receiving the highest dose of RF radiation had increased numbers of heart schwannomas. The female rats had increased numbers of brain gliomas. Based on these results, the lead author of the Ramazzini Institute study says that the IARC should consider changing its RF radiation designation from a possible human carcinogen to a probable human carcinogen.

However, Stephen Chanock, the director of the Division of Cancer Epidemiology and Genetics at the National Cancer Institute, is not so sure. The institute, which tracks the number of cancer cases nationwide, has been looking at changes in brain tumor rates since 2004. It has not found an uptick in the number of cases reported. "Cell phones have been around a long time," says Chanock. "We are by no means dismissing the evidence, and the Ramazzini study raises interesting questions. But it has to be factored in with other reports, and this is still work in progress."[20]

Cell phones have changed the habits of modern life—what people do during their downtime, how they work and study, and even how they walk and drive. The enormous amount of time people spend on their phones is having unintended consequences. Cell phone use is altering social interaction and communication; disrupting sleep; and may be triggering changes in brain function and cell growth. Technological progress often comes at a cost. The cost of using cell phones might be greater than anyone thought it would be.

CHAPTER TWO

The Dangers of Distraction

James Modisette was driving his black Camry on Interstate 35 in Denton, Texas, on Christmas Eve 2014 when he saw traffic stopped ahead. Beside him sat his wife, Bethany. In the back seat were their daughters, eight-year-old Isabella and five-year-old Moriah. A cautious driver, James slowed to a stop. Behind him, twenty-year-old Garrett Wilhelm was driving to his parents' home in his Toyota 4Runner. Cruising along at 65 miles per hour (105 kmh), Wilhelm was engaged in a video chat on his cell phone. He never saw the Modisettes' car ahead. He plowed into the back of the Camry at full speed. His sports utility vehicle rolled over the Modisettes' car, crushing the driver's side. Rescue workers had to extract James and also Moriah, who was buckled in a booster seat behind her father, from the wreckage. Moriah was airlifted to Cook Children's Hospital in nearby Fort Worth. She died from her injuries a short time later. James, Bethany, and Isabella were injured but survived.

Wilhelm admitted to police that he was using the FaceTime video chat app on his iPhone at the time of the crash. The police located his iPhone at the crash scene. The video call was still running. Wilhelm was indicted on manslaughter charges by a grand jury in Denton County. The case was scheduled to go to trial in 2019.

Long before the criminal case reached this point, the Modisettes had filed a lawsuit against Apple for damages, charging that the cell phone maker failed to install and implement a safer design. "At the time of the collision in question, the iPhone utilized by Wilhelm contained the necessary hardware (to be configured with software) to automatically disable or 'lock out' the ability to use [FaceTime]," states the lawsuit, which was filed in December 2016. "However, Apple failed to configure the iPhone to automatically 'lock out' the ability to utilize FaceTime while driving at highway speeds, despite having the technical capability to do so."[21]

Moriah Modisette was one of a rising number of people killed in accidents caused by cell phone distraction. While scientists are still evaluating the impact of cell phones on cancer and other physical diseases, public health officials already know the devices are affecting traffic accident rates, injuries, and deaths. Ironically, according to the National Highway Traffic Safety Administration (NHTSA), the number of US highway fatalities had steadily declined for forty years thanks to safer cars and the growth of public health programs to curb drunk driving. Then, in 2015, highway deaths increased by 8.4 percent—the largest percentage increase in one year since 1964. Ten percent of these fatal crashes were the result of distracted driving. A total of 476 people died in crashes caused by cell phone use—an increase of 25 percent over the number of such fatalities in 2011. The number of people killed in crashes on

Cell phone use while driving can have deadly consequences. In 2017 distracted driving played a role in 3,166 traffic deaths.

US roadways rose by another 5.6 percent in 2016. Fatalities in distraction-related crashes made up 9.2 percent of the total. Traffic fatalities decreased slightly in 2017, but distracted driving was still involved in 3,166 traffic deaths, or 8.5 percent of total fatalities.

Texting and Driving

Cell phone distraction is a factor in 25 percent of all car collisions, according to the Society for Risk Analysis, a nonprofit organization that promotes research into safety issues. But not all cell phone activities are equally dangerous. Talking on a cell phone increases crash risk by 2.2 times, but texting increases risk by 6.1 times. In a 2018 study published by the Society for Risk Analysis, researchers asked 447 drivers about how they viewed their driving abilities as well as how likely they were to talk on the phone and text while at the wheel. They found that a majority of drivers do not believe that texting while driving is dangerous. In fact, 68 percent of study participants reported needing "a lot of convincing" to believe in the dangers of texting and driving. Most drivers believe they can judge when it is appropriate to text while driving. However, the rising number of cell phone–related accidents suggests otherwise. "Drivers are not good at identifying where it is safe to use their phone,"[22] states Oscar Oviedo-Trespalacios, one of the authors of the study.

"Drivers are not good at identifying where it is safe to use their phone."[22]

—Oscar Oviedo-Trespalacios, a safety researcher at Queensland University of Technology in Brisbane, Australia

A survey by *Consumer Reports* also finds that a majority of drivers are convinced that they can handle a cell phone and drive safely. Fifty-two percent of all drivers in the *Consumer Reports* study admitted to engaging in distracting activities while driving. Forty-one percent said they used their hands to send a text message; 37 percent used their hands to play music on a smartphone; 20 percent used their hands to access a web browser or to compose, send, or read e-mail; and 8 percent watched videos on their phone while driving.

Cell phone distraction is an even bigger problem for younger drivers. Teen drivers are more easily distracted by their cell phones and are less likely to pull to the side of the road to use them. According to researchers at the NIH and Virginia Tech University, teen drivers are eight times more likely to crash or have a near miss when dialing a phone; seven to eight times more likely when reaching for a phone or other object; and four times more likely when texting. "My best friend always does that (uses smartphone) in the car," a British student told safety researchers

A Selfie Disaster in Portugal

In June 2018 a thirty-three-year-old Australian man named Michael Kearns and his thirty-seven-year-old partner, Louise Benson, originally from Bristol, England, traveled to Portugal to attend a friend's wedding and take a short vacation. During the early hours of June 12, the couple took a walk along a 100-foot-high (30 m) wall above Pescadores Beach in Ericeira, a surfing town on Portugal's western Atlantic Ocean coast. Later that morning, a beach cleaner found Kearns and Benson's lifeless bodies at the bottom of the wall. Nearby lay a cell phone. "Everything seems to indicate that the fall happened when they were probably trying to take a selfie," reported Rui Pereira da Terra, the head of the rescue service in the nearby port of Cascais.

Family and friends of the couple were devastated by the loss. "No words can describe what we have lost," a friend named Liz Catchpole wrote online. "Louise Benson you had a passion for life. . . . A quiet, not for long tho, Bristol girl who just loved life. Your smile infectious, your laugh amazing, your friendship invaluable. . . . In shock and speechless, you will be missed and I will miss you so much. Love you Lou, one in a million."

Pescadores Beach is a popular place to take photos, with countless tourists posting pictures of the beach and wall online. In a chilling twist, Kearns had posted a photo taken on the beach of a glass of red wine. In the background is the wall he would fall from less than twenty-four hours later.

Quoted in James Badcock, Helena Horton, and Henry Dyer, "'Selfie Death' as British Woman Plummets 30 Metres from Picturesque Sea Wall," *Telegraph*, June 13, 2018. www.telegraph.co.uk.

in 2018. "I am like . . . you are on Instagram. . . . What are you doing? You are going to kill me. I have to take her phone, I am holding your phone."[23]

Pedestrians in Danger

Pedestrian traffic deaths are also on the rise. Nearly six thousand pedestrians died in traffic accidents in 2017, according to the Governors Highway Safety Association (GHSA)—the highest number of pedestrian fatalities in twenty-five years. When asked why the number of pedestrian deaths was increasing, Maureen Vogel, a spokesperson for the GHSA, says, "One possibility can be seen during rush hour in downtown Chicago just by looking at both the drivers of the dozens of vehicles inching through traffic and the scores of pedestrians crossing the busy intersections. One thing many have in common is that their eyes are down, staring at their phones."[24]

Vogel's observation is supported by research conducted by investigators at Columbia University. A study of more than twenty thousand pedestrians at five different intersections in midtown Manhattan found that 42 percent of those who entered traffic during a "Don't Walk" signal were talking on a cell phone, wearing headphones, or looking down at an electronic device. "We are crazy distracted," says Melody Geraci, the deputy executive director of the Active Transportation Alliance, a nonprofit organization that advocates for better walking, cycling, and public transportation options. "After speeding and the failure to yield, distractions are the number three cause [of pedestrian fatalities], particularly by electronic devices."[25]

> "We are crazy distracted. After speeding and the failure to yield, distractions are the number three cause [of pedestrian fatalities], particularly by electronic devices."[25]
>
> —Melody Geraci, the deputy executive director of the Active Transportation Alliance

Excessive cell phone involvement can lead to other accidents, especially falls. In March 2018 a fifty-two-year-old woman fell fifteen stories from the balcony of her cruise ship cabin into the Atlantic Ocean when she lost her balance while taking a selfie. The ship's rescue team found the woman in the rough seas and pulled her to safety. She was lucky. A 2018 study conducted by researchers at the All India Institute of Medical Sciences in New Delhi, India, found that 259 people died while attempting to take selfies between October 2011 and November 2017. The phenomenon is growing. The researchers report that the number of selfie-related deaths increased from three in 2011 to thirteen in 2014, fifty in 2015, ninety-eight in 2016, and ninety-three in 2017. The large increase in the number of selfie deaths since 2014, the researchers write, "is because of increased usage of mobile phones, enhanced selfie features on mobile phones, increased availability of selfie sticks, and also promotion of the phenomenon of selfies through events like 'best selfie prize.'"[26]

The researchers believe the number of selfie-related deaths is probably a lot higher than they report. One reason for this is that they based their count only on reports in the news media, not on hospital records or any other sources, and they assume that not all selfie deaths appear in the news. Additionally, they only analyzed news reports that were written in English, meaning that selfie deaths that occurred in non-English-speaking countries were likely excluded from the count. "Although our study has enlisted the largest number of selfie deaths and incidents till date, this is just the tip of iceberg,"[27] they write.

There have been at least twelve more selfie deaths since the study concluded. On September 5, 2018, an eighteen-year-old Israeli tourist named Tomer Frankfurter slipped and fell 600 feet (183 m) while trying to take a selfie near the top of Nevada Falls, an iconic waterfall in Yosemite National Park. Two weeks later Tu Thanh Nguyen, a thirty-two-year-old woman from Sunnyvale, California, fell 200 feet (61 m) to her death while taking selfies at Pictured Rocks National Lakeshore on Michigan's Upper Peninsula.

Extreme Selfies

Many selfie deaths are the result of people trying to take a picture to impress their friends on social media. In October 2016 a twelve-year-old Russian girl named Oksana fell seventeen stories to her death from the railings of an apartment building balcony where she had climbed to take what is known as an extreme selfie. She sent the photograph to her best friend before losing her balance and falling. Seeing the picture, her friend called immediately to make sure Oksana was all right. She never answered. Oksana's uncle later posted this message on social media: "She was such a friendly girl. She was a good pupil, she

A man lies on a ledge to snap a selfie over the Grand Canyon. Since 2011 hundreds of people have lost their lives taking selfies, including such so-called extreme selfies.

had no problems at school. She took dance classes and English classes. She had so much to live for and now she has lost her life to the craze of looking to do extreme selfies for social media. There can be no other reason why she climbed over the damned handrail."[28]

Oksana's death was one of a growing number of selfie accidents involving the hazardous craze known as skywalking, which entails standing or walking atop very tall structures to get an extreme selfie. The more dangerous the image, the more followers the skywalker can accumulate on social media platforms like Instagram. A Russian man named Kirill Oreshkin has gained more than eighteen thousand followers on Instagram by posting stomach-churning selfies taken on the tops of buildings and towers. In pursuit of Instagram fame, Andrew Retrovsky, a seventeen-year-old student with more than eight thousand Instagram followers, attempted to take an extreme selfie while hanging from a rope from a nine-story building in 2015. The rope snapped, and Retrovsky fell to his death.

Railroad Accidents

Cell phone distraction has also been the cause of deadly train accidents. In 2016 a thirty-nine-year-old railway dispatcher caused the deadly collision of two trains in Germany because he was playing the game *Dragon Hunter 5* on his cell phone until just before the accident. The dispatcher admitted in court to setting the wrong train signals and failing to make an emergency call to the train drivers. Twelve people died and eighty-nine were injured. The dispatcher was sentenced to three and a half years in prison for involuntary manslaughter and bodily harm.

The deadliest US railroad accident of the twenty-first century was also the result of cell phone distraction, according to a National Transportation Safety Board (NTSB) report. In Los Angeles in 2008, engineer Robert Sanchez ran a red light while sending and receiving text messages on his cell phone. Seconds later, his crowded Metrolink commuter train crashed head-on with a Union Pacific freight train. "I saw it coming," said passenger Eric Forbes, who was riding in a car near the front of the train. "There was no

Which Teens Are Distracted Drivers?

Despina Stavrinos, a psychologist at the University of Alabama at Birmingham, wanted to learn which teens are at greatest risk of using cell phones while driving. So she asked forty-eight teens about their cell phone use while behind the wheel. She combined those results with the results of a personality test that breaks people into five groups. According to the personality test, people who score high on openness are willing to try new things; conscientious people follow through when they say they will; extraverts like to spend time with others; agreeable people are considerate of others; and neurotic people tend to be worriers.

Stavrinos expected to find that extroverts and people who are open and agreeable would be most likely to use their phones while driving. This turned out to be only partly correct. Teens who scored high on openness texted while driving more often than others did. However, extraverts were more likely to talk than to text. Stavrinos was surprised to find that agreeable teens use their phones less while driving than any other group. She suspects this is because agreeable teens "may be more likely to display cooperative, safety-relevant behaviors."

Another surprise was that conscientious teens were just as likely as open teens to use their phones while driving. Their tendency to follow through makes them feel the need to stay in touch with their friends, even while driving. "Teens should know that even their 'conscientious' friends may be distracted drivers," says Stavrinos. "No one seems to be 'immune' to distracted driving."

Quoted in Alison Pearce Stevens, "Here's What Puts Teen Drivers at Greatest Risk of a Crash," *Science News for Students*, October 11, 2018. www.sciencenewsforstudents.org.

time to stop," he said. "The next thing I knew I was in a seat in front of me. It was horrible."[29] The accident killed 25 people, including Sanchez, and injured 135.

Air Traffic Control

One of the worst places for cell phone distractions is in the air traffic control towers that direct more than one hundred thousand flights carrying 2.5 million passengers and crew each day worldwide. Nevertheless, such events do occur. A 2016 investigation of Federal Aviation Administration records by WABC News in New York found that between 2013 and 2016, twenty-six air traffic controllers nationwide were disciplined for cell phone use while directing planes. Air traffic controllers were reprimanded for texting, taking selfies, watching videos, and using Snapchat while

Cell phone use is so widespread that it has even been observed among air traffic controllers on the job. Between 2013 and 2016, twenty-six air traffic controllers nationwide were disciplined for cell phone use while directing planes.

on the job. One controller repeatedly used his cell phone for texting while guiding planes, including sending ten text messages in a two-hour period. "I would see people talking on the phone, I did see it many times. While they were working traffic," a retired air traffic controller told WABC. "You're responsible for what happens," said the retired controller. "How could you do anything that would be an obvious distraction?"[30]

In 2009 investigators found that an air traffic controller distracted by a cell phone contributed to a collision over the Hudson River between a helicopter and a small plane. An investigation by the NTSB found that air traffic controller Carlyle Turner, who was on duty at Teterboro Airport in New Jersey, missed a radio call from Steven Altman, the pilot of the small plane, because he was joking on his cell phone with a coworker about barbecuing a dead cat that had been found at the airport. "Fire up the cat,"[31] Turner said, according to a transcript of the call released by the NTSB. Altman, who had been in touch with Turner, was trying to confirm the correct radio frequency for the nearby Newark Airport, where another controller was trying to contact the pilot. In the call Turner did not hear, Altman read back the wrong radio frequency for the Newark Airport. As a result, Altman never spoke with the Newark controller, who was trying to warn him about the helicopter in his path. Shortly afterward, the two aircraft collided. All nine people aboard both aircraft were killed.

Cell phones are a relatively new invention, and people are still getting used to them. Safety experts hope that as the dangers associated with cell phone obsession and addiction become better known, people will learn to handle them more safely and cell phone makers will find ways to make them less distracting.

CHAPTER THREE

Troubling Changes in Communication and Social Interaction

Cell phones were designed to make communication easier and bring people together, but a growing body of research is showing that heavy cell phone use negatively affects social interaction and relationships. Many teens and young adults who have grown up in the age of cell phones say they prefer cell phone contact to face-to-face contact. They feel they have more control in cell phone messaging and are better able to present an image of themselves that they like. Some admit to using cell phones to avoid face-to-face interaction, preferring the busy solitude of texting, browsing, and partaking of music and videos as they choose. "I think we like our phones more than we like actual people,"[32] says Athena, a thirteen-year-old student.

Preventing Intimacy

Cell phones may be a good way to keep in touch with a large circle of friends, but they can be a barrier to meaningful conversations. Researchers at the Massachusetts Institute of Technology have found that people hold different face-to-face conversations when a cell phone is present. Believing they might be interrupted at any time, the participants in conversations with cell phones present do not discuss serious topics and do not reveal their deeper feelings. Since most people carry their cell phones with them at all times, this research suggests that the vast majority of conversations are becoming more superficial. "Our presence, our full attention is the most important thing we can give each other," says Nancy Colier, a psychotherapist and the author of the book *The Power of Off*. "Digital communications don't result in deeper connections, in feeling loved and supported."[33]

Many cell phone users have observed their relationships becoming more super-ficial since the advent of the cell phone.

E-mails have replaced letters, texts have replaced phone calls, and instant messaging has replaced face-to-face conversations. "The ritual of a weekly phone call with friends where there seemed like enough 'space' to talk about things in a meaningful way has eroded to texting to 'keep up,'" a professor at a leading techno-logical university told the Pew Research Center. "On the one hand, several of my friends feel more in touch because they are sharing memes, feel they are sharing witty things 'on the spot,' but there is less going into depth. We don't seem to be able to maintain both."[34] During these fleeting cell phone communications, people do not reveal much about their emotional lives. As a result even people who are good friends might remain unaware of a person's deepest hopes, fears, and troubles. The bond between people weakens to the point that when a person needs help or empathy, no one is there to give it.

Hearing but Not Listening

One of the reasons that many heavy cell phone users do not have meaningful face-to-face conversations is that they are dis-tracted by their cell phones. Being an attentive listener involves more than hearing the words the other person is saying. t also involves watching their facial expressions and body language for clues about how they are feeling. Looking at a cell phone during a conversation impairs a listener's ability to read facial expres-sions that provide important information about how the other person is feeling. Ineffective listening prevents deep, meaningful

conversations and is a barrier to intimacy. "Constant simultaneous communication leaves us lacking the ability to give one person our undivided attention, and if that one person is my wife or our kids, then I'm in some real trouble,"[35] says Chip Gaines, the costar of the television show *Fixer Upper*, who lost his cell phone and decided to stay unplugged for several weeks to reconnect with his family.

In addition, looking at a cell phone gives the impression that the listener is bored with the conversation and, more importantly, is uninterested in the speaker. "I think people have lost their ability to focus on the needs of others and really listen to another person because of how self-centric social media really is," one cell phone user told a focus group. "I think people have lost their ability to communicate in-person and have substantial conversations."[36]

Many parents and children believe that cell phone use is disrupting their ability to communicate. According to a Common Sense Media survey, 77 percent of parents feel that their teens get distracted by devices and do not pay attention when they are together. The feelings are mutual. Fully 41 percent of teens feel their parents are distracted by their devices and do not pay attention to them either. "Daddy," a fifteen-year-old girl said to her father when he took out his phone to look up a fact, "stop Googling. I want to talk to you."[37]

> "I think people have lost their ability to communicate in-person and have substantial conversations."[36]
>
> —A focus group participant at Nottingham Trent University

Creating Distance

Not being fully present in face-to-face conversations or even when just sitting together is eroding relationships between romantic partners. "It's not necessarily the top thing when my clients come in, but it's often in the mix, tied in with anxiety or insomnia or relationship issues," says British psychotherapist Hilda Burke. "Particularly when anxiety and insomnia's there, it's rare that it's not related in some way to heavy use of digital devices."[38] When one person is looking at a cell phone, the other person often refrains from interrupting them, even if they have something to say or simply want attention. This creates distance between the partners and is often a barrier to physical and emotional intimacy. "When you see your partner fully engrossed in their cell phone, it makes it feel like there's an even bigger gap that you have to jump over with your partner," says Vanessa Marin, a psychologist who specializes in couples therapy. "Pretty much every single couple I work with, internet and phone habits come up."[39]

Researchers James A. Roberts and Meredith E. David of Baylor University surveyed 145 adults about the effects of so-called phone snubbing, or phubbing, on romantic relationships. Phubbing occurs when a person uses or is distracted by a cell phone while in the company of his or her partner. The researchers found that phubbing creates conflicts over the use of cell phones, and these conflicts negatively affect overall satisfaction with the relationship. Dissatisfaction with the relationship in turn negatively affects an individual's feelings of well-being. "It is ironic that cell phones, originally designed as a communication tool, may actually hinder rather than foster satisfying relationships among romantic partners,"[40] write Roberts and David.

Cell phones also detract from conversations with larger groups, as when several students eat together at a restaurant or in a school dining hall. To avoid having everyone looking at their phones at the same time, some groups have an unspoken "rule of three," meaning that at least three people must be looking up from their phones and involved in conversation before a cell phone user looks down to check his or her phone. Although this technique keeps the conversation going, the face-to-face communication suffers. "I would say that conversations, well, they're pretty, well, fragmented," says Eleanor, a college student in New Hampshire who uses the rule of three. "Everybody is kind of in and out. Yeah, you have to say, 'What, what . . .' and sort of have people fill you in a bit when you drop out."[41]

Concerned About Conversation and Image

Many cell phone users say that they intentionally retreat into their digital world as a way of avoiding face-to-face conversations. "There is a certain amount of psychological anxiety involved with any social interaction and we can avoid that feeling by retreating into our device,"[42] explains Marguerite Summer, a psychologist in training. According to the Pew Research Center, 47 percent of smartphone owners ages eighteen to twenty-nine use their cell phones at least once a week to avoid social interaction.

Face-to-face conversations can be challenging for some people. Sherry Turkle, a sociologist at the Massachusetts Institute of

Technology, has found that many people prefer texting to talking in person because they are able to better control the conversation when they text. As one teenager told Turkle, face-to-face conversations are too spontaneous, free-flowing, and revealing. "What's wrong with conversation?" the teenager said. "I'll tell you what's wrong with conversation! It takes place in real time and you can't control what you're going to say."[43]

How a Cell Phone Obsession Can Wreak Havoc on a Relationship

In a July 2018 article in *Harper's Bazaar*, writer Carrie Battan describes how heavy cell phone use can strain a relationship:

> Like many of my friends, I get into frequent arguments with my boyfriend about our respective phone usage. To stare at an iPhone in front of a partner is to partake in some form of infidelity, whereby your attention is diverted from your loved one and redirected at hundreds of acquaintances and strangers. Sometimes I will catch myself actively siding with my phone over my boyfriend. . . .
>
> Another friend, Kelsea, . . . lives with her boyfriend, who teaches high school over an hour away. The pair use location-sharing on their devices. Sometimes, at night, if her boyfriend is later than usual, she'll check his location—only to find that it shows him sitting in front of the house in his car, neck craned. "He's just sitting there, on his phone," Kelsea says. "He's not responding to texts or anything—he's just looking at memes." In my relationship, the dynamic is reversed—I am the one constantly searching for down moments with my partner during which to check my phone. Sometimes I will catch myself lingering in the bathroom for an extra 20 minutes after I've brushed my teeth, idly scrolling through my social media feeds like a sugar addict digging through a pile of empty candy wrappers hoping to find scraps. "What were you doing?" my partner will ask when I've emerged, accusatorially. I can't even tell him, because I don't know.

Carrie Battan, "How to Escape the Seduction of Your Smartphone," *Harper's Bazaar*, July 27, 2018. www.harpersbazaar.com.

Heavy cell phone users also prefer digital connections because they are able to create and project an image of themselves that they like. "I spend my time online wanting to be seen as witty, intelligent, involved, and having the right ironic distance from everything," a thirty-four-year-old woman named Sharon told Turkle. "On Twitter, on Facebook, I'm geared toward showing my best self, showing me to be invulnerable or with as little vulnerability as possible."[44] Turkle describes the process of presenting an ideal image of oneself as self-curation, and she argues that it has corrosive effects on relationships. If people do not present all of themselves to their friends, they cannot receive the support and empathy that nourishes them emotionally. "Empathy requires that I get into your mental space, into your head, into your experience, and give you the comfort of knowing that I made that effort to listen and care, and that I'm taking responsibility for what I hear," says Turkle. "It's a commitment that we make to other people that involves us getting out of our own heads, and the constant self-curation online, the constant self-gratification of smartphones and social media, makes it harder for us to do this."[45]

Self-curating not only distorts the image that a person presents to others, but it also affects that person's self-image. Heavy cell phone users create such a positive image of themselves online that they are reluctant to have people see their authentic selves in face-to-face encounters. Gradually, they begin to see themselves based on how other people see them rather than as who they really are. "I worry that I'm giving up the responsibility for who I am to how other people see me," says Sharon. "You get lost in the performance."[46]

Nonstop Pressure

Self-curation and a dependence on approval from others is taking a psychic toll on young cell phone users, especially teenage girls, according to Twenge. "Social media levy a psychic tax on the teen doing the posting as well, as she anxiously awaits the affirmation of comments and likes," says Twenge. The sociologist describes

People who dislike face-to-face conversations may use their cell phones to avoid social interactions. Others prefer digital interactions because it allows them to create an ideal image of themselves that may not accurately reflect who they are in real life.

the anxiety expressed by a research subject she calls Athena. "When Athena posts pictures to Instagram, she told me, 'I'm nervous about what people think and are going to say. It sometimes bugs me when I don't get a certain amount of likes on a picture.'"[47] Twenge believes the nonstop pressures of cell phone use are affecting the mental health of people born between 1995 and 2012, which she calls iGen. She notes that according to the Centers for Disease Control (CDC), depressive symptoms increased by 21 percent for boys and 50 percent for girls between 2012 and 2015. The suicide rate also increased more among girls. Three times as many twelve- to fourteen-year-old girls killed themselves in 2015 as in 2007, compared with twice as many boys.

The CDC does not link rising levels of teen depression and suicide to cell phone use, but Twenge and her fellow researchers do. In a 2017 study published in *Clinical Psychological Science*, Twenge's team analyzed the cell phone habits of 506,820 adolescents in grades eight through twelve and national statistics on suicide deaths for those ages. The researchers found that 48 percent of young people who spent five or more hours a day on their cell phones had thought about suicide or made plans for it. That compares to just 28 percent of those who spent only one hour per day on their cell phones. The researchers found no other variables, including changes in the economy, family finances, or pressures from school that could account for the increase in mental health issues. "Although we can't say for sure that the growing use of smartphones caused the increase in mental health issues, that was by far the biggest change in teens' lives between 2010 and 2015,"[48] says Twenge.

The Antisocial Properties of Cell Phone Use

Researchers at Nottingham Trent University in Nottingham, England, interviewed twenty-one cell phone users in small groups, known as focus groups, to elicit experiences and perceptions about cell phone use. Two participants, identified as P2 and P6, described feeling rejected or upset when their friends became distracted from their face-to-face conversations by their cell phones:

P2: "I feel [it] personally. . . . Even if it's in a group and someone starts taking their phone out I feel like a sting of rejection, so I'll like sting them back. So I'm looking on my phone even if I've got no reason to. I'll just try and find a reason to look on my phone and then hope that they see that I don't need them either."

P6: "My partner absolutely drives me crazy on the phone. We go out for dinner . . . and he just sits there like that (mime sitting with phone in front). And that is all he does. And it is a nightmare going for dinner. And he never used to do it. All I can see is him like that (mime holding phone in front of face) constantly. It drives me mad."

Quoted in Daria J. Kuss et al., "Problematic Smartphone Use: Investigating Contemporary Experiences Using a Convergent Design," *International Journal of Environmental Research and Public Health*, January 2018. www.ncbi.nlm.nih.gov.

Twenge is not the only one to find a relationship between cell phone use and depression and suicide. The Monitoring the Future survey, funded by the National Institute on Drug Abuse, an agency of the federal government, has found that eighth graders who are heavy users of social media increase their risk of depression by 27 percent, and teens who spend three hours a day or more on electronic devices are 35 percent more likely to have a risk factor for suicide, such as making a suicide plan.

Over the past decade, the suicide rate has increased dramatically in all age groups, including teens. Suicide is now the second-leading cause of death of people ages ten to twenty-four, behind only accidental death. What role, if any, cell phone use plays in this public health crisis is still being debated. However, extensive research shows that heavy cell phone use is altering brain chemistry, triggering feelings of sadness, decreasing impulse control, and weakening the relationships between friends, family, and partners—the people who often can help a person planning a suicide to get the help they need.

> "Although we can't say for sure that the growing use of smartphones caused the increase in mental health issues, that was by far the biggest change in teens' lives between 2010 and 2015."[48]
>
> —Jean M. Twenge, a psychologist and researcher at San Diego State University

The cell phone was designed to connect people even when they are on the go. But it has evolved from a simple, mobile telephone into a full-time electronic companion, capable of serving up answers to questions, solutions to math problems, news, music, books, videos, games, live entertainment, and much more. For many, these electronic companions are so intriguing and alluring that they dominate the user's time and interest, leaving less opportunity and even desire for face-to-face interaction. In these instances, cell phones are driving people apart, eroding relationships, and increasing isolation rather than bringing people together.

CHAPTER FOUR

Cell Phones and the Brain

Cell phone addiction is similar to behavioral addictions that are recognized by the American Psychiatric Association (APA), including addictions to gambling and sex. Since behavioral addictions are associated with changes in the brain's chemistry and processing, researchers are interested in investigating the brains and thinking processes of cell phone users. This is especially true since there is a great deal of nonscientific, or anecdotal, evidence of changes in the mental health of cell phone users. There is growing scientific evidence that heavy cell phone use may have a negative and lasting impact on users' ability to think, remember, pay attention, and regulate emotion.

Brain Chemistry

Substance and behavioral addictions often affect chemicals in the brain known as neurotransmitters. These chemicals allow nerve cells, known as neurons, to transmit chemical messages to one another. Researchers from Korea University in Seoul wondered if heavy cell phone use affects neurotransmitters. To find out, they used brain imaging to compare the brains of nineteen teenage boys who were diagnosed with Internet or smartphone addiction with the same number of teenagers who were not addicted. They found that the brains of the addicted boys had significantly higher levels of gamma-aminobutyric acid (GABA), a neurotransmitter that slows brain signals, than they did glutamate-glutamine, a neurotransmitter that energizes brain signals. Energized brain signals help the brain concentrate. The results supported the observations of many parents and teachers who have noticed that heavy cell phone users seem to have trouble concentrating on tasks. "GABA slows down the neurons," explains Caglar Yildir-im, an assistant professor of human-computer interaction at the State University of New York at Oswego. "That results in poorer attention and control, which you don't want to have, because you want to stay focused. So that means you are more vulnerable to distractions."[49]

Distraction is one of the most important concerns regarding cell phone use because it contributes to traffic and pedestrian accidents, erodes relationships, and affects the work of students and workers. Although cell phone distraction has been observed in everyday life, scientists have tried to measure how great the effect is. Investigators at Florida State University wanted to know if cell phone notifications from incoming calls and text messages affected how people performed tasks. They found that although notifications are short in duration, they caused the mind to wander, which hurt performance on tasks. "We found that cellular phone notifications alone significantly disrupted performance on an attention-demanding task, even when participants did not directly interact with a mobile device during the task,"[50] explain the researchers. The amount of the distraction from the notifications was comparable to the amount observed when users actually used a mobile phone for voice calls or text messaging.

> "We found that cellular phone notifications alone significantly disrupted performance on an attention-demanding task, even when participants did not directly interact with a mobile device during the task."[50]
>
> —Cary Stothart, Ainsley Mitchum, and Courtney Yehert, researchers at Florida State University

Checking the cell phone is such a habit that investigators wondered if cell phone users would be distracted by their devices even without using them or receiving notifications. To find out, researchers at the McCombs School of Business at the University of Texas at Austin designed a unique experiment. They gave 548 participants two tests designed to measure their available brain power. One-third of the participants were asked to leave their cell phones outside the room. One-third were told to leave their cell phones face down at a certain place on their desks. The final third were told to leave their phones where they normally do, in their pockets or bags. All participants were told to turn their phones completely on silent, turning off the ring and vibrate so the cell phones would not make any sounds. The researchers found that the participants who left their phones outside the room performed better on the tests than did the participants who had their phones nearby. Those who left their phones in their bags or pockets outperformed those who could see their phones on their desks. The researchers believe that the participants with the cell phones nearby performed worse because they used part of their mental resources to ignore the phone. "Your conscious mind isn't thinking about your smartphone, but that process—the process of requiring yourself to not think about something—uses up some of your limited cognitive resources. It's a brain drain,"[51] explains Adrian Ward, one of the authors of the study.

> "Your conscious mind isn't thinking about your smartphone, but that process—the process of requiring yourself to not think about something—uses up some of your limited cognitive resources. It's a brain drain."[51]
>
> —Adrian Ward, a researcher at McCombs School of Business at the University of Texas at Austin

Impulse Control

Sociologists and psychologists have observed that many young people who are heavy cell phone users are, in general, prone to impulsive behavior. Researchers at Temple University wanted to see if such a connection really exists. To do so, they designed experiments to gauge impulse control and the willingness to wait for a better reward, known as delayed gratification. They administered the tests to ninety-one college students: sixty-five women and twenty-six men. They found that greater involvement with mobile devices correlates with a weaker tendency to delay gratifi-

42

Distracted walking can be just as dangerous as distracted driving. One study of pedestrians in Manhattan found that 42 percent of those who entered traffic during a "Don't Walk" signal were talking on a cell phone, wearing headphones, or looking down at an electronic device.

cation and a greater inclination toward impulsive behavior. "These findings lend some support to concerns that increased use of cell phones could have negative impacts on impulse control and the ability to appropriately valuate delayed rewards,"[52] write the researchers.

The research documenting how cell phone usage affects concentration and impulse control explains why many people use their cell phones while doing something else—listening to a lecture, watching television, and even participating in a conversation. Doing more than one thing at a time is known as multitasking. It is so commonplace among cell phone users that scientists have examined its effects on the brain.

"Smartphones encourage you to do multiple things at once, which is not physiologically healthy for you because we are not built to do a multitude of tasks at one time."[53]

—Clifford Nass, a professor of communications at Stanford University

Clifford Nass, a professor of communications at Stanford University, has found that multitasking is at odds with how the human brain has evolved and can be detrimental to its performance. "Smartphones encourage you to do multiple things at once, which is not physiologically healthy for you because we are not built to do a multitude of tasks at one time," says Nass. "Research shows that multitasking lessens your ability to focus on what is relevant. Your phone makes you feel like you have to respond, which then increases your stress and harms your cognitive thinking. Also, doing multiple tasks at once can make you jittery."[53]

Memory

The presence of the cell phone not only invites users to multitask but also encourages them to store data on the device rather than remembering it. This, too, is having an effect on the brain. Researchers in Russia have found that the expectation of having later access to information through a search engine makes people less inclined to store that information in long-term memory. The researchers call this process the Google Effect, but other researchers refer to it as digital amnesia. Similarly, reliance on cell phones for navigation has been shown to impair memory of routes and places.

Many people use their cell phones to take photographs of daily events, including where they go, what they eat, and who they are with, often looking at things only long enough to put them into the camera's viewfinder. Relying on the cell phone to record the scene, they do not spend a lot of time really observing things. Researchers at Fairfield University in Connecticut wondered if this behavior also brings about digital amnesia. They designed a study to find out if taking photographs of various life events impairs recall of those events. Participants in the study were given digital cameras and were taken on a tour of an art museum. They were told to take pictures of some objects on the tour but to observe other objects without taking a picture. One day later, the participants were tested on their ability to distinguish objects they had seen during the tour from brand-new objects. "The results showed that taking photographs diminished memory for observed objects," say three Temple University researchers who reviewed the Fairfield University study. "Specifically, the participants who used the camera during their tour showed a poorer ability to recognize objects as having been previously viewed." Since the practice of taking pictures

Multitaskers Use the Wrong Part of Their Brains

Professor Clifford Nass of Stanford University has found that people who do a lot of multitasking use a different part of their brains when they switch between tasks than do people who avoid multitasking. In his studies, he used functional magnetic resonance imaging (fMRI) equipment to monitor the brain activity of participants as they performed tasks and switched between them. The fMRI scans show that low multitaskers use a small area at the front of their brains, known as the prefrontal cortex, to switch tasks. This is an efficient use of the brain that enables the low multitaskers to perform tasks well. High multitaskers, by contrast, use a different part of their brains and do not perform as well. "High multi-taskers use approximately twenty times more of their brain than low multi-taskers do, and it's the wrong part. It's the visual cortex," says Nass. "They just turn their brains into overdrive when something switches. Not effectively. Not usefully. And because so much of their brain is active that doesn't help them, they do much worse on the tasks." Nass notes, however, that high multitaskers enjoy multitasking. "What this evidence suggests is that high multi-taskers just blithely use parts of their brains. They like their brains used, even if it's ineffective. That's why they fill their brains with so much stuff. That's why they multitask."

Stanford Alumni, "Multitasking: How It Is Changing the Way You and Your Children Think and Feel with Clifford Nass," YouTube, November 8, 2017. www.youtube.com.

and videos of trivial events is widespread due to the proliferation of cell phones, the Temple University researchers worry that large numbers of people are weakening their brains. They write, "If taking pictures can lead to weaker encoding of representations in memory, then this is an important facet of the cognitive impact of ubiquitous smartphone usage."[54]

Intelligence

Just as relying on cell phones impairs memory, so, too, does it decrease the initiative to think, according to researchers at Waterloo University in Ontario, Canada. In three studies involving 660 participants, the researchers tested various mental skills, such as verbal and math skills. The researchers found that students who are more intuitive and less analytical in general used the cell phones' search engines more often than the analytical students did. "They may look up information that they actually know or could easily learn, but are unwilling to make the effort to actually think about it," says Gordon Pennycook, one of the lead authors of the study. "Our research provides support for an association between heavy smartphone use and lowered intelligence."[55]

> "Our research provides support for an association between heavy smartphone use and lowered intelligence."[55]
>
> —Gordon Pennycook, a researcher at Waterloo University in Ontario, Canada

Researchers at Kent State University confirm Pennycook's observation. The researchers surveyed 536 undergraduate students about their cell phone use. They then looked at the grades of the students who participated in the survey. The researchers found that high cell phone use correlated with lower grade point averages (GPAs). "Cell phone use was significantly and negatively related to actual college GPA after controlling for demographic variables,"[56] the researchers concluded.

Addiction

The most worrisome impact of cell phone use on the brain is the possible development of a full-blown addiction. Cell phone addiction has been defined by researchers at the University of Oxford as "an inability to regulate one's use of the mobile phone, which eventually involves negative consequences in daily life (e.g. financial problems)."[57] In other words, addicted cell phone users are no longer in control of their cell phone use. Using it has become a compulsion. Cell phone addicts cannot resist engaging with the device even when they can see that it is harming their relationships, schoolwork or job performance, and even physical health and safety.

Early research indicates that cell phone addicts cannot simply give up the habit on their own or even with the help of apps that monitor use. "While various non-technical interventions, such as digital detoxes, and digital interventions, including apps to limit use, have been developed to help people control their smartphone use, none of these has proven to work yet,"[58] writes one

People who suffer from cell phone addiction are unable to control their mobile phone use despite experiencing negative consequences as a result. Like other addictions, cell phone addiction requires professional treatment.

group of researchers. The inability to stop a behavior without professional treatment is a definite sign of addiction.

The APA recognizes several behavioral addictions, but it does not yet list cell phone addiction in its *Diagnostic and Statistical Manual of Mental Disorders*, the book that sets the standard criteria for diagnosing mental disorders. Nevertheless, a survey of the psychiatric literature by researchers at the University of Madrid finds that most researchers agree that cell phone addiction is real: "There is a consensus about the existence of cell-phone addiction, but the delimitation and criteria used by various researchers vary."[59] The researchers point out that cell phone addiction shares some but not all of the characteristics of Internet addiction, another behavioral addiction that is widely accepted but is not yet included in the APA diagnostic manual. Like Internet addiction, cell phone addiction includes the possibility of escaping daily life and the ability to remain anonymous online. Unlike Internet addiction, cell phone addiction includes ease of access and the frequency of alerts and messages.

The most troubling aspect of cell phone addiction is how widespread it has become. It is a global phenomenon, as can be seen in the findings of various studies. Two studies, one in the United States and one in the United Kingdom, found that 66 percent of adults suffer from an irrational fear of being without a cell phone, known as nomophobia, short for "no-mobile-phone phobia." In the UK study, 41 percent of participants said they had two or more phones to make sure they stayed connected. Digital addiction expert Holland Haiis is not surprised. "Technological addiction can happen to anyone,"[60] she says.

A study conducted by researchers at the University of Maryland found that more than half of the college students in ten different countries who participated in the World Unplugged project could not go twenty-four hours without their cell phones. The World Unplugged project, an exercise to teach students about their cell phone use, was initiated by UNESCO, a United Nations

Students Experience Symptoms of Addiction When Deprived of Cell Phones

Participants in the World Unplugged project, in which students refrained from using their cell phones for twenty-four hours, described feeling addicted, anxious, and helpless without their cell phones. Some of the comments appear below.

- United Kingdom: "The only feeling I can relate to giving up my phone and Twitter is that of giving up smoking. . . . During the 24 hours of the experience I actually craved having my phone, and routinely checked my pockets for it every 5 minutes."

- United Kingdom: "The struggle I had, especially in the first few hours when I was on my own, could be described in the same terms as an addiction to alcohol. . . . Even actions such as eating breakfast had been shaped to such an extent that I was almost distressed when I couldn't read the news."

- United Kingdom: "It's like some kind of disorder, an addiction. . . . I starved myself for a full 15 hours and then had a full on binge. . . . I felt like there was no turning back now, it was pointless. I am addicted, I know it, I am not ashamed."

- China: "As time went by, my loneliness and helplessness spread, and the anxiety and desire of touching media became stronger."

- Slovakia: "That day I was very nervous, because I usually use my mobile as a 'touch think.' It means I take out my cell phone every minute and I look at the display, but I usually don't want to know the time or anything."

World Unplugged, "'Addicted' to Media," 2018. https://theworldunplugged.wordpress.com.

agency that focuses on education, science, and culture. According to the report, students around the world repeatedly used the term *addiction* to describe their dependence on their devices. These diverse students reported strikingly similar feelings when deprived of their cell phones, as demonstrated by these quotes from the report:

- "I was itching, like a crackhead, because I could not use my phone."

- "Media is my drug; without it I was lost. . . . I am an addict. I don't need alcohol, cocaine or any other derailing form of social depravity; I just need my drug. I had this somewhat hideous realization at about 7pm on Sunday, 24th October. I paced, I pondered the meaning of life and then I panicked. How could I survive 24 hours without it? How could I go on?"

- "Sometimes I felt 'dead.'"

- "I felt sad, lonely and depressed."[61]

The researchers concluded that "students' 'addiction' to media may not be clinically diagnosed, but the cravings sure seem real—as does the anxiety and the depression."[62]

Although extremely adaptable, the human brain is a delicate organ. Its functioning can be greatly affected by drugs, alcohol, disease, noise pollution, and many other external factors. Just as people wear a helmet to protect their brain when riding a bicycle or motorcycle, cell phone users must take steps to avoid injuring their brains with the small but powerful devices they hold in their hands.

CHAPTER FIVE

What Is Being Done About Cell Phone Overuse and Addiction?

From distracted driving to decreased brain function, cell phone addiction is affecting many areas of life—highways, schools, workplaces, and even the home. Public officials, educators, business leaders, technology experts, and health care professionals are only beginning to see cell phone overuse as a problem. A few are taking the first steps to address it. Public health officials are sounding warnings about the dangers of cell phone overuse. Legislators are passing laws to curb excessive cell phone use where it endangers lives. Technology companies are developing software to make the devices safer and to help addicted cell phone users kick the habit. And addiction treatment centers are gearing up to handle the influx of people seeking professional help to reclaim their lives.

Physical Health

The California Department of Public Health (CDPH) made headlines in December 2017 when it became the first state agency to issue guidance on how people could decrease their exposure to the RF energy emitted from cell phones. The recommended steps, such as keeping the phone away from the bed at night, are not what got media attention, however. Instead, headlines in *Time* and *Forbes* (for instance) focused on the suggestion that excessive cell phone use poses possible health hazards. When issuing its guidelines, the CDPH noted that some experts believe the RF energy emitted by cell phones can harm human health, specifically mentioning possible links between heavy cell phone use and some types of cancer.

Some critics thought the CDPH acted irresponsibly by linking cell phones and cancer since no tests have shown such a link. "The problem with a government body issuing guidelines on how to avoid something is that it implies the thing *should* be avoided," writes Sara Chodosh, an editor with *Popular Science*. "And there's no evidence that cell phones are dangerous to your health. Period."[63] However, in 2018 the NIH published its own large-scale studies, which found clear evidence linking RF radiation and heart tumors in male rats. Although the NIH studies do not prove a connection between cell phones and illness in humans, public health agencies are erring on the side of caution because they know how much time people today spend on their cell phones.

Some experts believe that excessive cell phone use is linked to certain types of cancer. Other experts dispute those claims.

Some heavy cell phone users are not waiting for action by public agencies. The 2017 ruling in Roberto Romeo's lawsuit against the makers of these devices focused global media attention on the possible link between heavy cell phone use and cancer. Lawsuits sometimes force manufacturers to change dangerous products. For example, the first cell phone cancer lawsuit, filed in 1992 by David Reynard against the cell phone manufacturer NEC and the carrier GTE Mobilnet, claimed that radiation from cell phones caused or accelerated the growth of a brain tumor in Reynard's wife, Susan, who was a heavy cell phone user. Reynard's lawsuit failed, but shortly afterward the Cellular Telecommunications Industry Association, an industry trade association, pledged $25 million for cell phone medical research. In addition, the Federal Communications Commission began to regulate RF emissions from cell phones. Similarly, after the car accident that claimed the life of Moriah Modisette, her parents sued Apple for not doing more to prevent heavy or addicted cell phone users from using apps while they drive. Although Apple denied any fault in this case, the cell phone maker did release its Do Not Disturb While Driving feature soon after the Modisettes filed the lawsuit.

Distracted Driving Remedies

The actions of the cell phone user who caused the crash that took Moriah Modisette's life and of many more like him have caused lawmakers in many states to take action against cell phone use while driving. At the time of the Modisette crash, Texas did not have a law against texting while driving. However, in May 2017 Texas enacted a statewide distracted-driving law that prohibits all texting and electronic messaging while driving, including e-mailing. Forty-seven states and the District of Columbia have laws that ban texting and other messaging while driving. Only Montana has no law banning texting and driving. Arizona and Missouri have partial bans. Many states—including California, Connecticut, Maryland, New Jersey, New York, Oregon, and Washington—have enacted laws banning the use of handheld cell phones while driving alto-gether. When the first cell phone laws were passed, law enforce-ment officers could only issue tickets for cell phone use to drivers who were pulled over for another reason, such as reckless driv-ing. Most states now allow police officers to pull over any driver simply for using a handheld cell phone, a policy known as primary enforcement.

Because studies have found that teen drivers are more eas-ily distracted while driving, most states have enacted special cell phone driving laws for new drivers—those with a learner's permit or who are younger than eighteen. These laws typically prohibit underage drivers from using a cell phone while operating a vehi-cle, including devices that are equipped with hands-free technol-ogy. Most of these states allow for primary enforcement of these laws as well.

Even though texting and other cell phone use during driving is outlawed in many states, a majority of drivers say they use their phones while driving anyway. Many of those drivers are among the estimated 38 percent of cell phone users who are addicted to their devices. Because of their compulsion to use their cell phones, addicts are not deterred by laws and fines. As a result, some cell phone makers and service providers realize that the only way to increase driver safety is to automatically disable cell phone features while the user is driving. For example, Apple's Do Not Disturb While Driving feature detects if the user is driving and automatically blocks notifications from appearing onscreen until the end of the journey. Preliminary studies show that cell phone use while driving decreased by 8 percent among those who had the feature activated, which is about 80 percent of users. A num-ber of third parties have created similar apps for Android devices. Some Internet service providers offer services that deactivate cell phones while driving, such as AT&T's DriveMode. These services block calls and text alerts but not notifications from apps.

Software developers are taking a similar approach to reduce railway accidents and deaths. A company named CellAntenna

Steps to Cut Back on Cell Phone Use

In a March 2018 paper published in *Digital Health*, researchers at the University of Oxford offer suggestions on how to treat cell phone addiction. They suggest that existing treatment programs for unrestrained gambling, shopping, and other addictive behaviors could be adapted to treat cell phone addiction:

> Behavioural approaches such as abstention (giving up) and moderating use (cutting down) as well as therapist-driven psychological approaches can be used. Smartphone use can be moderated in terms of the number of times a day a smartphone is used and how much time is spent (similarly to moderating calorie intake). Also, being conscious of emotions that make you want to check your phone and identifying which uses are not helpful, and focusing on moderating those can be helpful (similarly to focussing on nutrients that food provides). An experiment with a group of management consultants found that taking regular predictable time off from devices resulted in increased efficiency and collaboration, heightened job satisfaction, and a better work-life balance. . . .
>
> Several technical suggestions have been proposed to control use, such as: not always answering your phone by selectively turning off alerts; setting limits about not using a phone during certain situations or times; deleting old apps; unfollowing newsfeeds and friends that do not contribute usefully; and cleaning up email subscriptions.

Michelle H. van Velthoven, John Powell, and Georgina Powell, "Problematic Smartphone Use: Digital Approaches to an Emerging Public Health Problem," *Digital Health*, March 5, 2018. http://journals.sagepub.com.

has created a device called TrainSafe that detects when the driver of a train is calling or texting from the cab of the train engine. Activated by the cell phone's RF signal, TrainSafe immediately jams the call by releasing a burst of RF energy. Mindful of concerns about RF radiation and health, the makers of TrainSafe have designed the jamming module to activate only when it detects that a cell phone is attempting to connect with a cellular tower. The reactive jamming prevents the train engineer from being exposed to a constant jamming signal. Meanwhile, the National Transportation Safety Board has recommended that all rail companies install cameras and audio recorders at the controls so the companies can review whether their engineers are breaking cell phone rules.

Protecting Pedestrians

Cell phone addicts and other heavy cell phone users also use their devices while walking, making them a danger to themselves and to drivers who sometimes must take evasive action to avoid hitting them. Lawmakers are beginning to address this problem as well. In 2017, Honolulu, Hawaii, which leads the nation in pedestrian traffic deaths, became the first city in the United States to make it illegal for pedestrians to cross a street or highway while viewing a mobile electronic device. In March 2018 the city of Montclair in Southern California passed a law that bans pedestrians from viewing a mobile device or engaging in a cell phone call while crossing the street. The fine for the first offense is $100 and up to $200 for a second offense. Repeat offenders can be fined $500 for every additional offense within the year.

Cell phone overuse sometimes causes property damage when cell phone users bump into and damage objects. As a result, many museums now ban cell phones to prevent accidents that cause permanent damage to priceless works of art. One such museum is Lisbon's National Museum of Ancient Art, where a cell phone–wielding visitor knocked over a rare eighteenth-century statue while trying to take a selfie. In 2017, a visitor to the 14th Factory gallery in Los Angeles caused $200,000 worth of damage when

"We have plaster casts on ledges. If you're taking a photograph, you might back into them by mistake."[64]

—Tom Ryley, the communications officer of Sir John Soane's Museum in London she accidentally toppled a whole row of sculptures in the quest for a post-worthy selfie. Officials at Sir John Soane's Museum in London fear the same type of incident. "We have plaster casts on ledges," says Tom Ryley, the museum's communications officer. "If you're taking a photograph, you might back into them by mistake."[64] The Van Gogh Museum in Amsterdam, Netherlands, bans cell phone photography not only to protect the artworks but also because officials have found that taking pictures causes tension between those wishing to photograph and those wishing to view the paintings.

A growing number of landmarks are banning visitors from taking extreme selfies from dangerous locations. Authorities at Lake Tahoe, on the California-Nevada border, discourage visitors from taking any pictures of bears but especially selfies with their backs to the bears. "We've had mobs of people that are actually

A man poses for a selfie in a Croatian museum. Many museums now ban cell phone use because visitors have damaged priceless artworks by bumping into them while trying to take a selfie.

rushing toward the bears trying to get a 'selfie' photo," says Lisa Herron, a spokesperson for the Lake Tahoe Basin Management Unit. "It is presenting a safety issue. We are afraid someone is going to get attacked."[65]

Symptoms of Cell Phone Addiction

In an article for the online magazine *Medium*, Justin Baker, a product designer at Intuit and a founder of the California Association of Product Designers, summarizes the findings of researchers at the University of Madrid regarding the possible indicators of cell phone addiction:

- Conscious use of phones in dangerous situations or in prohibited contexts (e.g., while driving)

- Excessive phone use that causes social and family conflicts and confrontations, as well as loss of interest in other shared activities

- Continuing the behavior despite the negative effects and/or personal malaise it causes

- Excessive phone use causing noticeable physical, mental, social, work, or family disturbances (e.g., eye strain, symptoms of withdrawal, stress, and anxiety)

- Chronic impulsiveness to check a device

- Frequent and constant checking of phone in very brief periods of time causing insomnia and sleep disturbances

- Increase in use to achieve satisfaction or relaxation or to counteract a dysphoric mood

- Excessive use, urgency, need to be connected

- Need to respond immediately to messages, preferring the cell phone to personal contact

- Abstinence, dependence, craving

- Anxiety, irritability if cell phone is not accessible, feelings of unease when unable to use it

Justin Baker, "The Epidemic of Mobile Addiction: Signs, Symptoms, and Stats," *Medium*, October 15, 2017. https://medium.com.

Recognizing that cell phone addicts and heavy cell phone users will ignore laws and rules just as addicted drivers do, researchers at Carnegie Mellon University and the Indraprastha Institute of Information Technology in Delhi are trying to use technology to reduce extreme selfie deaths. They designed a cell phone app called Saftie that uses machine learning to identify when the image in the viewfinder represents a danger to the user. The software combines images, text, and GPS data to identify unsafe locations and then sounds an alarm to warn the user.

Fighting Addiction and Overuse with Apps

While some software developers are addressing symptoms of cell phone addiction and overuse, such as distracted driving, others are directly addressing the addiction. They are designing apps based on the principles of an addiction treatment known as cognitive behavioral therapy. This form of treatment aims to change addictive thoughts, feelings, and behaviors into healthy and positive ones. The apps highlight the cell phone user's negative habits and give the user options to change those habits. Some apps, for instance, allow the user to block access to certain websites and apps. Other apps show users how much time they are spending on social media sites and then enable them to set limits on their daily social media usage. These apps can be extremely helpful, explains Daria Kuss of Nottingham Trent University. "Raising awareness of one's own smartphone use can be the first step in the right direction of decreasing smartphone use," says Kuss. "Often, individuals are not aware of the frequency and extent of their smartphone use."[66]

> "Raising awareness of one's own smartphone use can be the first step in the right direction of decreasing smartphone use."[66]
>
> —Daria Kuss, a senior lecturer in psychology at Nottingham Trent University in Nottingham, England

Some software developers are creating apps intended to address cell phone addiction. Such apps may allow the user to block access to certain websites or set limits on daily social media usage.

Other apps use rewards to reinforce positive changes. One of these lets users set screen unlock and time-use goals and then rewards them with achievement badges when they meet their daily goals. The Norwegian app Hold even rewards student users by offering points for reducing their smartphone habit, which they can exchange for snacks and movie tickets. One app, App Detox, combines fitness with cell phone usage. In addition to time-based limitations, the app has an option that requires the user to walk in order to earn screen time.

Traditional Addiction Therapy

While apps may be useful to treat some forms of cell phone addiction, severe cases must be treated with therapies similar to those used to treat other behavioral addictions, including Internet addiction and gaming addiction. Treatment options include individual therapy, in which the therapist works with the user to address any underlying problems or co-occurring mental disorders that could be affecting cell phone use; face-to-face cognitive behavioral therapy; and motivational interviewing, which helps to find motivation to make a positive behavioral change. There are also treatment groups and centers, including Internet and Tech Addiction Anonymous, a twelve-step fellowship program similar to Alcoholics Anonymous; reStart, which offers six- to ten-week inpatient treatment programs to disconnect from digital media (such as the Internet, gaming, and cell phone use); and Camp Grounded, a kind of summer camp for adults that offers digital detox activities.

One of the problems with cell phone addiction is that it is virtually impossible to give up the devices on a long-term basis for the simple reason that, unlike drugs and alcohol, cell phones are a necessity of modern life. "The advantage of something like alcohol addiction is that you can stay away from bars; you can stay away from other drinkers; you can refrain from touching a drop of alcohol again," explains Hilarie Cash, the cofounder and chief clinical officer of reStart. "This is not that." Cash says that cell phone addiction, which almost always involves accessing the Internet excessively, is similar to an eating disorder because the client will always be exposed to the source of their addiction. The treatment technique is similar to that of eating disorders, as well. "Just as someone with an eating disorder has to learn how to avoid unhealthy foods that trigger their cycle, so, too, these clients have to learn to use the Internet in healthy ways and avoid things that will trigger their cycles,"[67] says Cash.

There is some hope that if cell phone users can give up their phones for at least a full day, they might become aware of their

> "I can't totally give up all my digital devices, but I'd like to have some unplugged days regularly."[69]
>
> —A participant in the Surviving a Day Without Smartphones project

cell phone habit and break it before it becomes a full-blown addiction. The organizers of the Surviving a Day Without Smartphones project discovered that some participants came away with a new understanding of their cell phone use and a desire to change their behavior. "Inspired by the project, several students have begun scheduling periods of respite when they pledge to be disconnected,"[68] explain the researchers. "I can't totally give up all my digital devices, but I'd like to have some unplugged days regularly,"[69] a male Chinese student wrote when the project concluded. A female Italian student reflected, "At the end of the day, I was missing neither social media nor having a digital connection. I was happy for the opportunity to challenge my unhealthy daily habits, because this gave me the opportunity to discover a slower, more conscious way."[70]

SOURCE NOTES

Introduction: A Growing Danger

1. Marcello Russo, Massimo Bergami, and Gabriele Morandin, "Surviving a Day Without Smartphones," *MIT Sloan Management Review*, Winter 2018, p. 8. www.mitsmr-ezine.com.
2. Quoted in Russo, Bergami, and Morandin, "Surviving a Day Without Smartphones," p. 8.
3. Quoted in Russo, Bergami, and Morandin, "Surviving a Day Without Smartphones," p. 8.
4. Quoted in Russo, Bergami, and Morandin, "Surviving a Day Without Smartphones," p. 8.
5. Quoted in Russo, Bergami, and Morandin, "Surviving a Day Without Smartphones," p. 8.
6. Quoted in Russo, Bergami, and Morandin, "Surviving a Day Without Smartphones," p. 8.
7. Quoted in Daria J. Kuss et al., "Problematic Smartphone Use: Investigating Contemporary Experiences Using a Convergent Design," *International Journal of Environmental Research and Public Health*, January 2018. www.ncbi.nlm.nih.gov.
8. Jean M. Twenge, "Have Smartphones Destroyed a Generation?," *Atlantic*, September 2017. www.theatlantic.com.
9. Quoted in Camila Domonoske, "Pedestrian Fatalities Remain at 25-Year High for Second Year in a Row," NPR, February 28, 2018. www.npr.org.
10. Michelle H. van Velthoven, John Powell, and Georgina Powell, "Problematic Smartphone Use: Digital Approaches to an Emerging Public Health Problem," Digital Health, March 5, 2018. http://journals.sagepub.com.

Chapter One: The Making of a Public Health Crisis

11. Quoted in Paul Lewis, "'Our Minds Can Be Hijacked': The Tech Insiders Who Fear a Smartphone Dystopia," *Guardian*, December 12, 2017. www.theguardian.com.

12. Quoted in Alice G. Walton, "Phone Addiction Is Real—and So Are Its Mental Health Risks," *Forbes*, December 11, 2017. www.forbes.com.
13. Jane E. Brody, "Hooked on Our Smartphones," *New York Times*, January 9, 2017. www.nytimes.com.
14. Quoted in Lewis, "'Our Minds Can Be Hijacked.'"
15. Michael Winnick, "Putting a Finger on Our Phone Obsession," *dscout Blog*, June 16, 2016. https://blog.dscout.com.
16. Erica Kenney and Steven Gortmaker, "United States Adolescents' Television, Computer, Videogame, Smartphone, and Tablet Use: Associations with Sugary Drinks, Sleep, Physical Activity, and Obesity," *Journal of Pediatrics*, March 2017, p. 144. www.ncbi.nlm.nih.gov.
17. Sylvie Royant-Parola et al., "The Use of Social Media Modifies Teenagers' Sleep-Related Behavior," *L'Encéphale*, June 8, 2017. www.ncbi.nlm.nih.gov.
18. Yanfie Xie et al., "Spinal Kinematics During Smartphone Texting—a Comparison Between Young Adults with and Without Chronic Neck-Shoulder Pain," *Applied Ergonomics*, April 2018. www.ncbi.nlm.nih.gov.
19. Quoted in Agence France-Presse, "Italian Court Rules Mobile Phone Use Caused Brain Tumour," *Guardian*, April 21, 2017. www.theguardian.com.
20. Quoted in Charles Schmidt, "New Studies Link Cell Phone Radiation with Cancer," *Scientific American*, March 29, 2018. www.scientificamerican.com.

Chapter Two: The Dangers of Distraction

21. Quoted in 6ABC, "Family Sues Apple, Claims FaceTime Distracted Driver in Fatal Crash," January 3, 2017. https://6abc .com.
22. Quoted in Society for Risk Analysis, "Majority of Drivers Don't Believe Texting While Driving Is Dangerous," Cision, July 11, 2018. www.prnewswire.com.

23. Quoted in Daria J. Kuss et al., "Problematic Smartphone Use: Investigating Contemporary Experiences Using a Convergent Design."

24. Quoted in Domonoske, "Pedestrian Fatalities Remain at 25-Year High for Second Year in a Row."

25. Quoted in Domonoske, "Pedestrian Fatalities Remain at 25-Year High for Second Year in a Row."

26. Agam Bansal et al., "Selfies: A Boon or Bane?," *Journal of Family Medicine and Primary Care*, July/August 2018. www.ncbi.nlm.nih.gov.

27. Agam Bansal et al., "Selfies."

28. Quoted in Keyan Milanian, "Schoolgirl Plunges 17 Floors to Her Death After Sending 'Extreme Selfie' to Her Best Friend," *Mirror*, November 18, 2016. www.mirror.co.uk.

29. Quoted in Joel Rubin, Ann M. Simmons, and Mitchell Landsberg, "'Total Destruction': At Least 17 Die in Head-On Metrolink Crash," *Los Angeles Times*, September 13, 2008. www.latimes.com.

30. Quoted in Jim Hoffer, "Investigators Exclusive: Air Traffic Controllers Texting While Directing Planes," WABC-TV, February 4, 2016. https://abc7ny.com.

31. Quoted in Laura Italiano and Bruce Golding, "Fury as Air Traffic Controller in 2009 Crash Returns to Work," *New York Post*, May 5, 2014. https://nypost.com.

Chapter Three: Troubling Changes in Communication and Social Interaction

32. Quoted in Twenge, "Have Smartphones Destroyed a Generation?"

33. Quoted in Brody, "Hooked on Our Smartphones."

34. Quoted in Janna Anderson and Lee Rainie, "Stories from Experts About the Impact of Digital Life," Pew Research Center, July 3, 2018. www.pewinternet.org.

35. Quoted in Megan Stein, "Chip Gaines Reveals the 'Miserable' Experiment That Sometimes Forced Wife Joanna to 'Bear the Load,'" *People*, February 9, 2018. https://people.com.
36. Quoted in Anderson and Rainie, "Stories from Experts About the Impact of Digital Life."
37. Quoted in Sherry Turkle, "Stop Googling. Let's Talk," *New York Times*, September 26, 2015. www.nytimes.com.
38. Quoted in Stuart Dredge, "Mobile Phone Addiction? It's Time to Take Back Control," *Guardian*, January 27, 2018. www.theguardian.com.
39. Quoted in Carrie Battan, "How to Escape the Seduction of Your Smartphone," *Harper's Bazaar*, July 27, 2018. www.harpersbazaar.com.
40. James A. Roberts and Meredith E. David, "My Life Has Become a Major Distraction from My Cell Phone: Partner Phubbing and Relationship Satisfaction Among Romantic Partners," *Computers in Human Behavior*, January 2016. www.researchgate.net/publication/282763744_My_life_has _become_a_major_distraction_from_my_cell_phone_Part ner_phubbing_and_relationship_satisfaction_among_roman tic_partners.
41. Quoted in Sherry Turkle, *Reclaiming Conversation: The Power of Talk in a Digital Age*. New York: Penguin, 2015, pp. 20–21.
42. Quoted in Elizabeth Segran, "The Case Against Smartphones," *Fast Company*, August 15, 2014. www.fastcompany.com.
43. Quoted in Turkle, *Reclaiming Conversation*, p. 24.
44. Quoted in Turkle, *Reclaiming Conversation*, p. 24.
45. Quoted in Sean Illing, "How We're Becoming Slaves to Technology, Explained by an MIT Sociologist," Vox, March 27, 2018. www.vox.com.
46. Quoted in Turkle, *Reclaiming Conversation*, p. 24.
47. Twenge, "Have Smartphones Destroyed a Generation?"
48. Quoted in Walton, "Phone Addiction Is Real."

49. Quoted in Sandee LaMotte, "Smartphone Addiction Could Be Changing Your Brain," CNN, December 1, 2017. https://edition.cnn.com.

50. Cary Stothart, Ainsley Mitchum, and Courtney Yehert, "The Attentional Cost of Receiving a Cell Phone Notification," *Journal of Experimental Psychology Human Perception & Performance*, June 29, 2015. www.ncbi.nlm.nih.gov.

51. Quoted in Christopher Bergland, "Are Smartphones Making Us Stupid?," *Athlete's Way* (blog), *Psychology Today*, June 25, 2017. www.psychologytoday.com.

52. Henry H. Wilmer and Jason M. Chein, "Mobile Technology Habits: Patterns of Association Among Device Usage, Intertemporal Preference, Impulse Control, and Reward Sensitivity," *Psychonomic Bulletin & Review*, October 2016. https://link.springer.com.

53. Quoted in Julie Croteau, "Smartphone Users: Beware," Be-Well Stanford, 2016. https://bewell.stanford.edu.

54. Henry H. Wilmer, Lauren E. Sherman, and Jason M. Chein, "Smartphones and Cognition: A Review of Research Exploring the Links between Mobile Technology Habits and Cognitive Functioning," *Frontiers in Psychology*, April 25, 2017. www.ncbi.nlm.nih.gov.

55. Quoted in Waterloo University, "Reliance on Smartphones Linked to Lazy Thinking," Waterloo News, March 5, 2016. https://uwaterloo.ca.

56. Andrew Lepp, Jacob E. Barkley, and Aryn C. Karpinski, "The Relationship Between Cell Phone Use and Academic Performance in a Sample of U.S. College Students," *SAGE Open*, January–March 2015. http://journals.sagepub.com.

57. Van Velthoven, Powell, and Powell, "Problematic Smartphone Use."

58. Van Velthoven, Powell, and Powell, "Problematic Smartphone Use."

59. José De Sola Gutiérrez, Fernando Rodríguez de Fonseca, and Gabriel Rubio, "Cell-Phone Addiction: A Review," *Frontiers in Psychiatry*, October 24, 2016. www.ncbi.nlm.nih.gov.

60. Quoted in Kelly Wallace, "Half of Teens Think They're Addicted to Their Smartphones," CNN, July 29, 2016. http://edition.cnn.com.

61. Quoted in World Unplugged, "Going 24 Hours Without Media," 2018. https://theworldunplugged.wordpress.com.

62. World Unplugged, "Going 24 Hours Without Media."

Chapter Five: What Is Being Done About Cell Phone Overuse and Addiction?

63. Sara Chodosh, "There's No Evidence That Cell Phones Pose a Public Health Risk, No Matter What California Says," *Popular Science*, December 19, 2017. www.popsci.com.

64. Quoted in James Tarmy, "Selfie Culture Has Some Art Museums Caving on Strict No-Photo Policies," *New Haven Register*, October 1, 2018. www.nhregister.com.

65. Quoted in Emma Cueto, "Lake Tahoe Officials Ban Bear Selfies in Effort to Get Tourists to Stop Risking Their Lives," *Bustle*, October 31, 2015. www.bustle.com.

66. Quoted in Dredge, "Mobile Phone Addiction?"

67. Molly Young, "What an Internet Rehabilitation Program Is Really Like," *Allure*, January 21, 2018. www.allure.com.

68. Russo, Bergami, and Morandin, "Surviving a Day Without Smartphones."

69. Quoted in Russo, Bergami, and Morandin, "Surviving a Day Without Smartphones."

70. Quoted in Russo, Bergami, and Morandin, "Surviving a Day Without Smartphones."

Center for Safe and Responsible Internet Use
474 W. Twenty-Ninth Ave.
Eugene, OR 97405
website: www.cyberbully.org

The Center for Safe and Responsible Internet Use helps young people keep themselves safe and respect others on the Internet. Its website contains information designed to help people learn about responsible Internet behavior.

Childnet International
Studio 14, Brockley Cross Business Centre
96 Endwell Rd.
London SE4 2PD
website: www.childnet.com

Childnet International's mission is to work in partnership with others around the world to help make the Internet a safe place for children. Its website features news; projects; general safety advice for parents, young people, and teachers; links; and other information.

Common Sense Media
650 Townsend, Suite 435
San Francisco, CA 94103
website: www.commonsensemedia.org

Common Sense Media is an independent nonprofit organization that provides education, ratings, and tools to families to promote safe technology and media for children and teens. Its goal is to help kids thrive in a world of media and technology.

Get Net Wise
website: www.getnetwise.org

Get Net Wise is a website provided by Internet industry corporations and public interest organizations. Its goal is to ensure that Internet users have safe and constructive online experiences. The website contains information about youth safety, security, and privacy.

Pew Research Center
1615 L St. NW, Suite 700
Washington, DC 20036
website: http://pewinternet.org

Through its Pew Internet & American Life Project, the center studies how Americans use the Internet and how digital technologies are shaping the world today. Its website has the results of numerous studies about privacy and the Internet.

Special Interest Group on Computer-Human Interaction (SIGCHI)
119 E. Union St., Suite A
Pasadena, CA 91103
website: www.sigchi.org

SIGCHI is an international society for professionals, academics, and students who are interested in human-technology and human-computer interaction. A subgroup of the Association for Computing Machinery, the organization offers publications, hosts message boards, and holds conferences in the multidisciplinary field of human-computer interaction.

Stay Safe Online
website: www.staysafeonline.org

Part of the National Cyber Security Alliance, this website offers educational materials, information for home users on protecting their computers and protecting their children, cybersecurity practices, videos, a self-assessment quiz, and additional information.

ZDNet
www.zdnet.com/topic/mobility

ZDNet provides news coverage and analysis on technology trends. Its "Mobility" section discusses how wireless carriers, machine-to-machine connections, and new devices are affecting productivity.

Books

Lisa J. Amstutz, *Smartphones*. Mendota Heights, MN: North Star, 2017.

Nicholas Kardaras, *Glow Kids: How Screen Addiction Is Hijacking Our Kids—and How to Break the Trance*. New York: St. Martin's Griffin, 2017.

Brian Merchant, *One Device: The Secret History of the iPhone*. New York: Little, Brown, 2017.

Bradley Steffens, *Thinking Critically: Cell Phones*. San Diego: ReferencePoint, 2018.

Jean M. Twenge, *iGen: Why Today's Super-Connected Kids Are Growing Up Less Rebellious, More Tolerant, Less Happy—and Completely Unprepared for Adulthood*. New York: Atria, 2017.

Internet Sources

Janna Anderson and Lee Rainie, "Stories from Experts About the Impact of Digital Life," Pew Research Center, July 3, 2018. www .pewinternet.org.

Carrie Battan, "How to Escape the Seduction of Your Smartphone," *Harper's Bazaar*, July 27, 2018. www.harpersbazaar .com.

Jane E. Brody, "Hooked on Our Smartphones," *New York Times*, January 9, 2017. www.nytimes.com.

Paul Lewis, "'Our Minds Can Be Hijacked': The Tech Insiders Who Fear a Smartphone Dystopia," *Guardian*, December 12, 2017. www.theguardian.com.

Charles Schmidt, "New Studies Link Cell Phone Radiation with Cancer," *Scientific American*, March 29, 2018. www.scientific american.com.

Jean M. Twenge, "Have Smartphones Destroyed a Generation?," *Atlantic*, September 2017. www.theatlantic.com.

Michael Winnick, "Putting a Finger on Our Phone Obsession," *dscout Blog*, June 16, 2016. https://blog.dscout.com.

INDEX

ABOUT THE AUTHOR

Bradley Steffens is a poet, a novelist, and an award-winning author of more than forty nonfiction books for children and young adults.